THE FEAST DAYS

OF YAH

BY : BRITTANI RAMIREZ

YAH'S BIBLICAL FEAST DAYS

FEAST DAY INDEX

Yah's special feast days are made very special by Him! Only He can say what is really, really special and holy. Here's a little map to find all of His special days mentioned in this book.

OUR WONDERFUL BIBLE IS LIKE A TREASURE CHEST, PACKED WITH AMAZING STORIES AND IMPORTANT LESSONS THAT SHOW US HOW MUCH YAH LOVES AND CARES FOR US. INSIDE THIS SPECIAL BOOK, YAH HAS SHARED WITH US SOME VERY SPECIAL DAYS TO CELEBRATE - THESE ARE THE BIBLICAL FEASTS. THEY'RE NOT JUST ANY DAYS; THEY ARE SUPER SPECIAL TIMES FILLED WITH HAPPINESS, MEMORIES, AND DEEP MEANING.

EACH FEAST IS LIKE A SPECIAL PRESENT FROM YAH, HIS WAY OF ASKING US TO COME CLOSER AND GET TO KNOW HIM BETTER. THEY ARE CHANCES FOR US TO TAKE A BREAK FROM OUR EVERYDAY STUFF, TO CELEBRATE ALL THE GOOD THINGS HE DOES, REMEMBER THE GREAT THINGS HE HAS DONE, AND THINK ABOUT WHAT HE TEACHES US.

THE SABBATH (SHABBAT)

"SHABBAT" (שַׁבָּת)
MEANS "REST" OR "CEASING."

As we embark on this exciting journey through these special days, we will learn why and how we celebrate them. We'll discover how each feast ties into the grand story of love and redemption, from the freedom of the Israelites from Egypt to the sacrificial love of The Messiah.

So let's begin this journey with open hearts and joyful spirits, as we delve into the beautiful traditions of the Biblical feasts. Together, we'll uncover the meanings behind these celebrations and discover how they can bring us even closer to Yah's loving presence in our lives.

"We begin our festive journey with the Sabbath, a unique day that occurs every seventh day, marking a rhythm in our week. Picture a beautiful dance, with six days of movement and action, and then a day of rest, just like a pause in music that adds depth to the melody.

Remember when Yah created the world? He crafted the sun and moon, stars and planets, the land and the sea, animals and humans - everything around us. But on the seventh day, Yah did something different. After six days of shaping the universe, He rested. But why would Yah, who never gets tired, rest? Let's uncover this mystery! (Genesis 2:2-3).

Yah didn't need to rest because He was tired. Instead, He wanted to set a special example for us. He created the Sabbath as a day of rest and remembrance, a day to step away from our usual tasks, to remember and celebrate His wonderful creation. It's as if Yah is saying, 'Pause and look around. Appreciate the world I have created for you. Isn't it beautiful?'

On this day, we cease our work, just like Yah did. It's not just about not doing our jobs or homework, though. It's about resting our minds and spirits, refreshing ourselves for the coming week. It's a chance to appreciate the beauty of Yah's creation that we often miss in our busy lives.

Sabbath is also a special time to gather with those we love. Imagine it as a weekly family reunion where we connect with our family, share stories, pray together, and express our love for each other and for Yah. It's like a weekly holiday that Yah has given us to enjoy!

So, each Sabbath, let's remember to rest, reflect, and rejoice, celebrating Yah's creation, and cherishing the time we spend with our loved ones.

PASSOVER (PESACH)

(פֶּסַח) "PASACH"
MEANING"TO PASS OVER" OR "TO SPARE."

Next in our festive journey, we encounter Passover, a feast rich with history and spiritual significance. This special celebration marks an incredible event that took place thousands of years ago, when Yah intervened in a miraculous way to save the Israelites from harsh slavery in Egypt (Exodus 12:13-14).

Imagine a night filled with anticipation, the Israelites huddled in their homes, a special meal prepared, and their bags packed for a journey they've been awaiting for so long. This was the first Passover night. They painted their doorposts with the blood of a lamb, following Yah's command, and that night, something extraordinary happened.

Yah protected each house marked with the lamb's blood, saving His people from a terrible plague. This was their sign of freedom, the moment they had been released from the chains of their oppressors!

This historic event carries a powerful message, one that reverberates beyond that ancient time and reaches us today. The lamb's blood on the doorposts wasn't just a one-time sign; it was a symbol of protection and salvation that would echo throughout history.

Enter The Messiah, who is referred to as our 'Passover Lamb.' But why is that? Well, just like the original Passover lamb's blood saved the Israelites, Yahusha's sacrifice saves us from a different kind of bondage - the bondage of sin. By offering Himself, Yahusha has provided a way for us to be freed from our wrongdoings and to be reconciled with Yah.

So, every year, as we sit down for the Passover meal, we remember that night in Egypt when Yah set His people free. We recall the bitterness of slavery through the bitter herbs and the sweetness of freedom through the wine and matzah. And as we do, we also remember Yahusha, our Passover Lamb, and the freedom He has won for us. It's a powerful time of reflection and gratitude, a moment to thank Yah for His deliverance - past, present, and future.

FEAST OF UNLEAVENED BREAD
"CHAG HAMATZOT" (חַג הַמַצּוֹת)

"MEANS "FEAST" OR "FESTIVAL (CHAG) חַ
הַמַצּוֹת (HAMATZOT) REFERS TO "UNLEAVENED BREAD"

Right after the monumental event of Passover, another significant celebration takes place, called the Feast of Unleavened Bread. This feast is so closely tied to Passover that sometimes people refer to the entire eight-day period as Passover. But the Feast of Unleavened Bread is its own unique celebration with its special traditions and deep spiritual symbolism.

For seven days, the bread we eat is a bit different - it's flat, without yeast, and it's called unleavened bread or 'matzah.' This isn't just a dietary change; it has a powerful historical and spiritual significance. Do you remember the story of the Israelites' exodus from Egypt? They had to leave in such a hurry that they didn't have time to wait for their bread to rise, so they baked it without yeast (Exodus 12:15-20).

Every time we eat the unleavened bread during this feast, we're reminded of the Israelites' hasty departure from Egypt. We imagine the mixed feelings of fear and excitement they must have felt as they stepped into their newfound freedom, guided by Yah's mighty hand.

But there's more to this unleavened bread than meets the eye. In the Bible, yeast often symbolizes sin and corruption, because just like yeast causes dough to rise, sin can grow and spread if we allow it. By removing yeast from our bread during this feast, we symbolize the removal of sin from our lives. It's a time of self-examination, a call to purge any wrong thoughts, attitudes, or actions, and to seek Yah's forgiveness and purification.

So, as we enjoy the Feast of Unleavened Bread, we not only remember the dramatic escape of the Israelites from Egypt, but we also reflect on our personal journey to eliminate sin from our lives which also is a reminder of Yahs mercy. We commit to live as a people set free, not just from physical slavery, but from the spiritual slavery of sin, walking in the light of Yah's truth and love."

FEAST OF FIRST FRUITS

"CHAG HABIKKURIM" (חַג הַבִּכּוּרִים)

חַג (CHAG) MEANS "FEAST" OR "FESTIVAL" IN HEBREW.
הַבִּכּוּרִים (HABIKKURIM) REFERS TO "FIRST FRUITS"

The Feast of First Fruits is like a breath of fresh spring air in our festive journey. Falling just after Passover and the Feast of Unleavened Bread, it's a time of new beginnings and renewed gratitude. It's an occasion for thanking Yah for His abundant blessings, specifically the first harvest of the year (Leviticus 23:10-14).

In ancient times, people depended directly on the land for their food. They sowed seeds, prayed for rain, and waited in hope for a successful harvest. The first ripe grains were a sign of Yah's provision and faithfulness, the first evidence that there would be enough food for the year.

On this day, people brought a sheaf (a bundle of harvested grain stalks or stems bound together for drying or storage purposes.) of this first harvest to the priest, who waved it before Yah in a special ceremony. It was their way of saying, 'Thank you, Yah, for the food we eat. We recognize that every good thing we have comes from you.' Even today, as we may not farm the land ourselves, it's a beautiful moment to appreciate all of Yah's provisions in our lives.

But the Feast of First Fruits isn't only about thanking Yah for physical food. It has a deeper spiritual significance connected to our Messiah.

Many people share a fascinating story about Yahusha, suggesting that, on this special day, he might have risen from the dead, making him our first fruit! Wouldn't that be cool!

What does this mean? Just as the first fruits are a promise of the harvest to come, Yahusha's resurrection is a promise of our future resurrection and eternal life. Yahusha, being the first one to rise from the dead never to die again, has paved the way for us. Through Him, we have the hope of eternal life.

So, as we celebrate the Feast of First Fruits, we rejoice in Yah's physical and spiritual provisions. We're reminded of His faithfulness in providing for our daily needs, and we celebrate the glorious promise of eternal life through Yahusha, our 'first fruit' of resurrection.

COMMANDMENTS

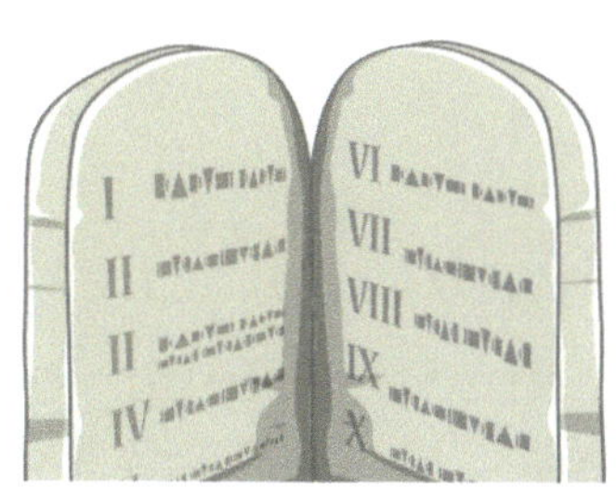

FEAST OF WEEKS/ PENTACOST

"CHAG HABIKKURIM" (חַג הַבִּכּוּרִים)

"SHAVUOT" (שָׁבוּעוֹת)
MEANING "WEEKS."

Now, let's journey together to another exciting feast, the Feast of Weeks, also known as Pentecost. Have you ever noticed that this feast has two names? The name 'Feast of Weeks' is because this feast takes place seven weeks, or a 'week of weeks,' after the Feast of First Fruits. 'Pentecost' comes from a Greek word meaning fiftieth, as it's celebrated on the fiftieth day.

This joyous feast marks the end of the grain harvest season. It's a time of overflowing thankfulness when we acknowledge Yah's generous provision. The Israelites celebrated this day by bringing offerings from their new harvest to Yah (Leviticus 23:15-21). They would wave two loaves of bread made from the new wheat harvest before Yah, expressing their gratitude for His blessings.

But Pentecost isn't just about agricultural harvest; it's a day of spiritual significance, too. On this day, something extraordinary happened at Mount Sinai. Do you remember when Moses received the Ten Commandments from Yah? That historic event took place on Pentecost! So, while we're expressing our gratitude for Yah's provision, we're also celebrating the gift of His law, a guiding light for our lives.

Fast forward many years later to a room in Jerusalem. The Messiah's disciples were gathered together on the day of Pentecost, and the Holy Spirit descended upon them in a powerful way (Acts 2:1-4). This was the beginning of a new chapter in Yah's story, where His Spirit would dwell in His people, guiding and empowering them.

So, during the Feast of Weeks, or Pentecost, we rejoice in Yah's physical provision and celebrate the spiritual gifts He has given us: His law and His Spirit. It's a time of thanksgiving and a time of reflection on the extraordinary ways Yah interacts with His people, guiding and nourishing us, body and soul.

FEAST OF TRUMPETS
"YOM TERUAH" (יום תרועה)

יום (YOM) MEANS "DAY."
תרועה (TERUAH) MEANS "SHOUTING" OR "BLASTING
(OF THE SHOFAR)."

Can you hear the shofar's call? It heralds the arrival of Yom Teruah, the Day of Shouting or Blasting. This day, set apart in the seventh month of the Biblical calendar, is ordained in Leviticus 23:24 as a time for a sacred assembly commemorated with the blowing of trumpets. Unlike the Gregorian calendar that marks the new year in January, Yom Teruah is observed according to the Biblical timeline, serving as a day of remembrance through the sounding of the shofar.

The shofar, traditionally a ram's horn, is the quintessential symbol of this day. Its blast is not merely a call to celebration but a stirring summons to reflection and repentance. This sound is a multi-faceted symbol; it is a call to awaken the soul, a reminder of our covenant with the Divine, and a prompt for personal and communal introspection. On Yom Teruah, the sound of the shofar resonates deeply, marking a time for renewal and spiritual realignment as we enter another cycle of the year.

But the shofar carries a deeper, more awe-inspiring significance. It heralds a future filled with hope and anticipation, as foretold in the Scriptures. The Bible promises that one day, the Messiah will return, and what will signal this momentous event? A loud call of the shofar! (1 Thessalonians 4:16-17).

Just imagine that day, when the sound of the shofar will fill the skies, louder and clearer than anything we've ever heard before. With that divine blast, the Messiah will return, ushering in an era of peace and righteousness unlike any before. This future expectation enriches the shofar's blast with layers of spiritual anticipation, connecting the present to the prophetic visions of redemption and renewal.

So, every time we observe Yom Teruah, when the shofar's sound echoes in our ears, we do more than mark the start of a new cycle. We also remind ourselves of the promise of the Messiah's return. Each blast of the shofar fills us with hope and anticipation, stirring our hearts to live in a manner pleasing to Elohim as we eagerly await the Messiah's glorious return. This observance connects the rhythm of our yearly calendar with the profound spiritual anticipation of redemption, making each sounding of the shofar a moment of deep reflection and joyful expectation.

DAY OF ATONEMENT
"YOM HAKIPPURIM" (יוֹם הַכִּפֻּרִים)

יוֹם (YOM) MEANS "DAY"
הַכִּפֻּרִים (HAKIPPURIM) COMES FROM THE ROOT WORD
"KIPPUR," WHICH MEANS "TO ATONE" OR "TO CLEANSE."

Following the joyful noise of the Feast of Trumpets, we come to a more solemn and introspective time in our festive journey - the Day of Atonement, also known as Yom Kippur. While it may seem more somber, this day holds profound significance and an essential message of hope for all of us (Leviticus 23:26-32).

The Day of Atonement is a day of repentance, a day of reconciliation, a day when we come before Yah with humility and honesty, acknowledging our mistakes, our shortcomings, and our sins. It's a day when we seek Yah's forgiveness and pray for the strength to turn away from actions and attitudes that don't honor Him.

But why is it called 'Day of Atonement'? In Biblical times, this was the only day of the year when the High Priest would enter the Most Holy Place in the temple to make a special sacrifice for the sins of the people. It was a day of profound significance, an opportunity for the entire community to be cleansed and reconciled with Yah. (Leviticus 16)

Fast forward to our times, we no longer offer animal sacrifices as in the days of old, but the Day of Atonement is still a powerful reminder of the great sacrifice made for us - not by a human high priest, but by Yahusha Hamachiach Himself. Yahusha, who is our High Priest, offered Himself as the perfect and ultimate sacrifice for our sins, bringing us into a renewed covenant with Yah.

By His selfless act, Yahusha has made it possible for us to be forgiven and to enjoy a close relationship with Yah. His sacrifice opened the way for us to approach Yah with confidence.

So, on Yom Kippur, we express our deep sorrow for our sins, but we also rejoice in The Messiah's incredible love and grace. It's a day of reverence and gratitude, a day to reflect on our actions, and to renew our commitment to living a life that honors Yah, thankful for the forgiveness and redemption we have through Messiah!

FEAST OF TABERNACLES
(סֻכּוֹת) "SUKKOT"

סֻכּוֹת (SUKKOT) IS THE PLURAL FORM OF THE HEBREW WORD סֻכָּה (SUKKAH), WHICH MEANS "BOOTH" OR "TABERNACLE."

Finally, our journey through the biblical feasts brings us to the Feast of Tabernacles, or Sukkot. This feast is a joyful culmination of the holy celebrations, a time of thanksgiving and remembrance, and a grand celebration of Yah's faithful care and provision (Leviticus 23:33-44).

Sukkot lasts for seven days, and it's a feast like no other. During this time, families build and dwell in temporary huts or booths, known as 'sukkahs.' These aren't just for decoration, though. They are a vivid reminder of the temporary shelters that the Israelites lived in during their 40-year journey in the wilderness.

As we sit in our sukkahs, we recall those long-ago days when Yah's chosen people were wandering in the desert, guided by a pillar of cloud by day and a pillar of fire by night. Despite the harsh conditions, Yah was with them every step of the way, providing food, water, and protection.

And just like Yah was with the Israelites in the wilderness, He is with us in our journey through life. He provides for our needs, guides our paths, and watches over us with love and care. As we celebrate Sukkot, we rejoice in His faithfulness and express our trust in His continuous protection, provision and mercy.

Moreover, Sukkot reminds us that our time on earth is temporary, much like the sukkahs we dwell in. Our permanent home is with Yah, in the kingdom that He has prepared for us. This feast, therefore, is also a time to look forward with joy and anticipation to the day when we will dwell with Yah forever, in a place where His tabernacle is with His people (Revelation 21:3).

So, as we celebrate the Feast of Tabernacles, let's rejoice in Yah's presence, provision, and promises. Let's dwell in His love, give thanks for His blessings, and look forward to the day when we will tabernacle with Him forever.

These biblical feasts form a beautiful tradition, a living history that connects us with Yah and with our Messiah Himself. They are more than just days marked on a calendar - they are rich experiences that help us remember Yah's love and the incredible gift of The Messiah's sacrifice.

When we celebrate the Sabbath, we are reminded of Yah's design for rest and refreshment, a holy pause in the rhythm of life that Yahusha Himself observed. With Passover, we recall the deliverance of the Israelites and see a powerful picture of our own deliverance from sin through The Messiah, our Passover Lamb.

The Feast of Unleavened Bread prompts us to remove the 'yeast' of sin from our lives, just as Yahusha lived a sinless life. Celebrating the Feast of First Fruits, we thank Yah for His provision and rejoice in Yahusha's resurrection, the promise of our future resurrection.

Pentecost brings gratitude for Yah's spiritual gifts - His law and His Holy Spirit - given to guide us, empower us, and mark us as His. The Feast of Trumpets echoes with the joyful sound of new beginnings and the thrilling anticipation of Yahusha's return.

The Day of Atonement is a poignant time of repentance and reconciliation, reminding us of the forgiveness we have through Yahusha, our High Priest and the ultimate sacrifice. And finally, the Feast of Tabernacles fills us with joy and thankfulness for Yah's continual presence, protection, and provision, while also pointing us forward to the day when we will dwell with Him forever.

So, as we celebrate these feasts, we're not just recalling events from the past. We're joining in a story that spans thousands of years, a story that includes the Israelites, Yahusha, and us. We're participating in traditions that Yahusha Himself observed. And as we do, we deepen our understanding of His love, His work, and His plans. We draw closer to Him, growing in our relationship with Yah, and strengthening our faith.

Let's cherish these feasts, dear children, as precious gifts from Yah. As we journey through each celebration, let's remember the wonderful truths they teach us, give thanks for Yah's incredible love, and draw closer to Him in joy and faith.

LETS DIVE IN TO SOME WORDS

GLOSSARY

Some of the names and terms in this book may be different than you are used to. Here are some definitions and explanations of these words and terms used in this book

ATONEMENT:

Making amends for sin or wrongdoing, traditionally observed with prayer, fasting, reflection.

BLEMISH:

Symbolizes imperfection; in sacrifices, animals without blemish represent purity.

CRUCIFIXION:

Yahusha's execution, symbolizing sacrifice for redemption of sin.

ELOHIM:

Hebrew for "God," representing divine power or the supreme being.

FEAST:

Religious festival or celebration commemorating an event in the bible or aspect of Yah's relationship with His people.

MESSIAH:

Anointed one," savior or liberator, specifically Yahusha as the awaited savior.

YAH:

Also known as Yahuah, Yahweh or Yahovah, the personal name of the God of Israel. (𐤀𐤉𐤀𐤌)

YAHUSHA:

The Messiah, also known as Jesus or Yeshua, signifying the savior providing salvation to humanity. The son of 𐤀𐤉𐤀𐤌

SUPPORTING SCRIPTURES

WHAT DOES THE BIBLE SAY?

Here are some beautiful and powerful scriptures about keeping Yah's feasts ad laws!

EXODUS 12:14-17

"This will be a day for you to remember and celebrate as a festival to 𐤉𐤄𐤅𐤄; from generation to generation you are to celebrate it by a perpetual regulation."

LEVITICUS 23:1-44

"𐤉𐤄𐤅𐤄 said to Moshe, 'Speak to the people of Isra'el and say to them: "The designated times of 𐤉𐤄𐤅𐤄 which you are to proclaim as holy convocations are my designated times."'"

PSALM 119:1-8

"How happy are those whose way of life is blameless, who live by the Torah of 𐤉𐤄𐤅𐤄!"

EXODUS 31:13

"You are to speak to the people of Isra'el and say, 'Above all, you are to keep my Shabbats; for this is a sign between me and you through all your generations; that you will know that I am 𐤉𐤄𐤅𐤄, who sets you apart for me.'"

NEHEMIAH 8:1-12

"They found written in the Torah, which 𐤉𐤄𐤅𐤄 had commanded through Moshe, that the people of Isra'el were to live in sukkot during the feast of the seventh month."

DEUTERONOMY 8:6

"Therefore you shall keep the commandments of 𐤉𐤄𐤅𐤄 your Elohim, to walk in His ways and to fear Him."

LETS DIVE IN TO SOME QUESTIONS

FUN QUESTIONS AND ACTIVITIES

Here are some engaging activities and questions to ponder and discuss with your family or friends, inspired by the insights we've gathered from this book!

SHABBAT

QUESTION: Why do you think Yah wants us to rest on the Sabbath?
ACTIVITY: Plan a special Sabbath meal with your family, where everyone contributes to the cooking and setting the table. During the meal, share one thing from the past week you are thankful for.

PASSOVER

QUESTION: How is Yahusha like the Passover lamb?
ACTIVITY: Draw a picture showing how the Israelites painted the doorposts of their homes with the lamb's blood. Explain to your family what this image represents.

FEAST OF UNLEAVENED BREAD

QUESTION: Why do you think yeast is used as a symbol for sin in the Bible?
ACTIVITY: Bake unleavened bread with your family, and while doing it, discuss the importance of removing sin from our lives.

FEAST OF FIRST FRUITS

QUESTION: Why do you think the first fruits were offered to Yah?
ACTIVITY: Plant a seed and watch it grow. As it sprouts and bears fruit, discuss how Yahusha's resurrection promises us new life.

LETS DIVE IN TO SOME QUESTIONS

FUN QUESTIONS AND ACTIVITIES

Here are some engaging activities and questions to ponder and discuss with your family or friends, inspired by the insights we've gathered from this book!

FEAST OF TRUMPETS

QUESTION: How do you feel when you think about Yahusha's return?
ACTIVITY: Make a paper trumpet and decorate it. As you blow your trumpet, remember the joyous return of Yahusha that we look forward to.

DAY OF ATONEMENT

QUESTION: Why is it important to ask Yah for forgiveness and to forgive others?
ACTIVITY: Write a letter to Yah, confessing any wrongdoings and asking for forgiveness. Remember, Yahusha has made it possible for us to be forgiven!

FEAST OF TABERNACLES

QUESTION: How does it make you feel to know that Yah is always with us, protecting us?
ACTIVITY: Build a small model of a sukkah with craft supplies. As you create it, think about how Yah protected the Israelites in the wilderness, and how He protects and guides us today.

I hope these insights inspire further questions and activities related to the wonderful feasts of Yah and His Torah!